Jagged Little Thoughts

Miranda Crispin

BookLeaf Publishing

India | USA | UK

Presentation by *BookLeaf Publishing*

Web: www.bookleafpub.com

E-mail: info@bookleafpub.com

ISBN : 9789357447713

First edition 2021

DEDICATION

To myself. May I find my passion again.

Drowning

Do people know I'm drowning?
Does anybody care?
How could they see me flailing
Wrapped in their own despair.

Black Dog

There's a black dog you see
Always following me
The darkened beast lurking
Just behind me smirking.

Sometimes he's big, and sometimes he's small
Sometimes I can barely see him at all.
But just when I think that he's gone for good
He comes back bigger than any dog should.

He snarls and he bites and he rips and he roars,
And gathers my memories all up in his jaws.
Tainting what little good I had left
He gleefully reminds me of my flaws.

I try not to listen, like I know I should.
"You're useless, you're ugly, and you're just no
damn good."
Just pretend it's okay, there's nothing wrong.
Hands over my ears, and try to stay strong.

Slowly but surely his words do sink in,
I know I can't fight him, I know I can't win.
He pants on me with a foul smelling breath,
As I curl in a ball and just wait for death.

He'll be right there with me,
Till the day I die.
That miserable beast,
My black dog and I.

Pain

And no I can't share my pain
Because what if it infects your brain
Like a parasite it does creep
Keeping me away from my sleep

I couldn't do that to another
Take your mind like a lover
It'll be all you can think about
Do nothing but scream and shout

So no you can't have my pain
More victims for it to drain
Through my veins it does seep
Maybe now I'll take that leap.

Piss off, you prick

Piss off you prick
Pretending you're better
You make me sick
Better than me

You use me like a toy
Make me care before
Taking away the joy
Power over me

I should have known
Trusting you was a mistake
No love you've shown
Curse this heart

Say you don't care
It can't hurt me anymore
The words we don't share
Rot in my mouth

So piss off you prick
As my heart you unpick
Without even knowing
Save me the heartache

Morality

What's the point of even trying,
when we're all just slowly dying?

Vampire

When I said I loved you, you coiled away,
Like a vampire runs from the light of day.
With your words you broke my heart to pieces,
Still my love for you never falters, never ceases.

What am I?

What am I?
Always average
Never the best
Put this lousy soul to rest

Why do I bother?
No-one notices
And no-one cares
These silent words I bare

Who will love me?
so broken and ruined
a worthless skin
my own patience grows thin

Why be strong?
waste time fighting
and I'm already broken
words that can never be spoken

It's not worth trying
I'm no longer afraid
I'll die quietly here
while you feel betrayed

Thoughts

Some of you don't know
and some of you won't care
but I have things within me
things that I need to share

A lot of things have happened
things that no-one could foresee
all of this has changed my life
and permanently damaged me

Years burying and suffering
until no more I could cram
all this has made me question
question who i am

Who is this girl so unsure?
the one who cries to sleep
her heart so broken up and torn
still your secrets i will keep

I don't want to let you go
but I'm scared to keep you near
my heart loves you but still
I'm filled with such a fear

Is it better to let go?
let us both be done
go our separate ways
that way neither has won

So do i stay or do i go?
To stay is to slowly die
not even knowing who i am
but shouldn't I at least try?

Future

Am I the only one that feels the pendulum swinging?
My heart beat's so loud that my ears are ringing.
I can feel time passing like sand through a sieve.
My heart and my soul, I have nothing more to give.
You'll continue being silly, and I'm glad you're having fun,
But I'm scared about the future and I'm not the only one.

Spoken word

And it was then I knew. I knew that we were done.
I had loved you, like I was the earth and you were the sun.

I know exactly what did it, I know why it's broken.
But there are some things that just can't be unspoken.

You did something so foul and it just blows my mind,
So without even thinking I did something just as foul in kind.

And it's not something that I can get past,
just because you said we could last.

Why should I pay for a mistake that you made?
You gambled with a life that was not yours to trade.

So it's time to split the bill and cash the chips in.
I won't stay and be prisoner to your sin.

Pen

The pen may be mightier than the sword but
both have limitations,
but if you really want
to be heard
use both without hesitation.

Rain

Darkness falls all around
Pounding down like rain
But it can start things anew
and wash away the pain.

Despite

Not every tunnel has a light

Not every story turns out right

There's not a cure to every blight

Some people hurt you out of spite

Not every soul is pure and white

Not only darkest in the night

Not every fighter wants to fight

Not all dreams can take their flight

Sometimes things just aren't alright

Even when you hold them tight

Not every person knows your plight

But we try our hardest with all our might

Mistake

You were a Mistake.
Not a small mistake, or a mis-take, or a
whoopsie.
Nor an accident, or an error.
A Mistake:
An act or judgement that was misguided or
wrong.
Cold, hard, uncaring Mistake.
Broken heart caused by a Mistake.
But we learn from Mistakes.
And we don't make them again.

Just a thought...

Do not give up and please do not fret,
The flow of words will come soon I'll bet.
You may have troubles, and you may have
doubts
But there are stories in you, just let them come
out!

Justice

Justice
I scoff at the word.
Fake words designed to calm fake people!
Are you happy?
Did you get your pound of flesh?
Good. Now get out.
My heart breaks in panicked sobs
Did he die?
No. But he may as well have.

Time Haiku

Am I not dead yet?
Time stands still yet runs so fast
So soon to the ground

Hope

You've been running for so long and you've
done so well,
I know how many times you've wanted out of
this hell.
It seems like an eternity, you're just trying to
survive
But see here's your chance to finally thrive!

So now I'll just stop, but I wanted you to know,
No matter how far you've come or how far to
go,
I'll be right there with you, and you won't be
afraid
You can finally find peace here with me in the
shade.

Depression is something that haunts everyone
And I can say from experience it isn't much fun.
But hang in there baby, it gets better, it's true!
And your family and friends are all there for
you.

Love

Do not worry love
Love will find you when ready to
Just be patient, wait

9 789357 447713